Companion Figures

A Visual Aid for Teaching

Modern Jews Engage the New Testament

Enhancing Jewish Well-Being in a Christian Environment

Rabbi Michael J. Cook, PhD

Companion Figures

A Visual Aid for Teaching

Modern Jews Engage the New Testament

Enhancing Jewish Well-Being in a Christian Environment

Rabbi Michael J. Cook, PhD

For People of All Faiths, All Backgrounds
JEWISH LIGHTS Publishing

Modern Jews Engage the New Testament Companion Figures:
A Visual Aid for Teaching

2008 Paperback, First Printing
©2008 by Michael J. Cook

For People of All Faiths, All Backgrounds
Published by Jewish Lights Publishing
www.jewishlights.com

ISBN 978-1-58023-393-4 (Pbk.)
ISBN 978-1-68336-549-5 (Hardcover)

Contents

Contents

Introduction

As an instructional aid, this booklet, *Companion Figures*, reproduces the eighty-four charts and diagrams from *Modern Jews Engage the New Testament: Enhancing Jewish Well-Being in a Christian Environment* (Jewish Lights).

Why were these "Figures" in that book itself? Visual learning can valuably complement what is absorbed from basic reading. These pictorials stimulate attention, simplify concepts, and facilitate and reinforce the recall of information and approaches vital to enhancing Jewish well-being in a Christian environment. Many also provide ready recourse to those New Testament passages discussed in the book—readers do not need to look these up on their own (or skip doing so given the inconvenience). Above all, "Gospel Dynamics," the primary emphasis of *Modern Jews Engage the New Testament* (pp. 83–91), are more readily comprehended when laid out in diagrammatic fashion.

Why reproduce these pictorials here in *Companion Figures*? This booklet can be employed as the focus of group instruction and discussion—whether in adult education or conversion classes; synagogue clergy institutes; ministerial association meetings; presentations at interfaith centers for Jewish-Christian learning; seminary or college courses; and the like. Participants first can be assigned specified pages in the full book; thereafter they can bring *Companion Figures* alone to class (or instructors can keep the copies and distribute them as sessions begin).

Planners of sessions should consult the "Suitability Index" (*Modern Jews Engage the New Testament*, pp. 300–302) for programming ideas, and then, scanning the "List of Figures" (pp. 303–305), select those that can best enhance their teaching sessions or group discussions. Or they can consult the sample programs constructed below—accommodating them to suit instructional taste. Teachers are advised first to read *Modern Jews Engage the New Testament* in its entirety to make certain that they can understand the text's overall aims, interrelate its spectrum of subjects, and field the wide variety of questions they will likely be asked. Especially vital is that they closely review all entries in the "Notes on Terminology—Keeping Our Referents Straight" (pp. xviii-xxiv).

- As a reminder of the numbering scheme of each "Figure" (e.g., *"Fig. 5.3"*): the first numeral indicates the chapter where the Figure is displayed in *Modern Jews Engage the New Testament*; the second where, in the sequence of pictorials in that chapter, a given Figure appears.
- In the sample programs below, page assignments often come with superscripts that will help readers to more quickly locate the material listed:

t	=	top of page
m	=	middle of page
b	=	bottom of page
n	=	endnote

Using *Companion Figures* for A SINGLE (i.e., Isolated) Discussion Session

These are among those "Figures" which best lend themselves to this kind of program.

Figures to Display	Subject Addressed	Pages to Assign in Advance from *Modern Jews Engage the New Testament*	
		Some Basic Material	Additional Preparation
1.1 (*also 11.2*)	Fundamental questions Jews find hard to answer	xviii–xxiv, 4–11, 54^m–57, 128-130 (321$^{n.6}$), 255–263	69–72, 104^b–105, 106^b–108, 131^m–132^m, 154^b–159^m
4.1–2	Christianity's emergence	33–39	68^m–69^m, 71^b–72, 261^b–263^m, 275^b–276
3.3; 5.1–8	Jesus in the land of Israel	xxiii^b–xxiv, 20–21^t, 40–57, 316$^{n.20}$	75–82, 91, 124–125, 132^m, 269^m
10.1–3	The Last Supper & Passover	109–117, 320$^{n.10}$	118–120, 176^m
12.1–5, 8–10	The impact of Passion traditions on the Jewish people	5^m, 90, 121–132	133–148, 295^m, 321$^{n.6}$
22.1–2 (also 12.1–5; 15.5; 16.2–7; 18.1)	Is the New Testament anti-Jewish/Semitic?	122^m, 195–202, 219–229, 278–88	134^m–140, 172^b–175^t, 186–188^t, 206^b–208, 213–217, 275^m

Using *Companion Figures* for MULTI-SESSION Discussion Series

These four suggested courses lend themselves to being:

- shortened (by omitting sessions)
- expanded (by extending sessions)
- combined (by stringing one course to another)

The courses are sequenced in *increasing* sophistication.

Course #1: New Testament Basics Jews Should Know

(5 sessions)

Session	Figures to Display	Subject Addressed	Pages to Assign in Advance from *Modern Jews Engage* ...	
			Some Basic Material	Additional Preparation
1st	*3.1–10*	Introductory factors	18–29	271[b]–277
2nd	*4.1–2*	Early configurations of Christianity	33–39	68[m]–69[m], 71[b]–72, 216[m]–217[t], 258[m], 261[b]–263[m], 275[b]–276
3rd	*5.1–7*	Jesus in the land of Israel	40–57, 316[n.20]	12–13[m], 75–80, 124–125, 132[m], 317[nn.30–31], 317–318[n.12]
4th	*4.1–2; 6.1–6*	Paul in his Diaspora context	33–35, 58–72, 163–175, 269–271	18–19, 21[m], 155–156
5th	*8.1–5*	"Gospel Dynamics"	83–91, 289[b]–292[t], 352–354	75–82, 132, 188–189, 208, 297[t]

Course #2: How Christian Holy Days Impact the Jews

(5 sessions)

Session	Figures to Display	Subject Addressed	Pages to Assign in Advance from *Modern Jews Engage the New Testament*	
			Some Basic Material	Additional Preparation
1st	*9.1–5*	Christmas	95–108, 319[nn.2–5, 8–10], 320[nn.11–12, 14]	14[m], 40[m]–41, 53[m], 63b–64[t], 210[b], 260[t]
2nd	*10.1–3; 15.3; 21.1*	"Maundy" Thursday	109–120, 274[m]	178[m], 181[m]–183[t], 321[n.13]
3rd	*11.1–2*	Good Friday	121–132, 321[nn.4,8], 322[nn.9–10]	xx, 90–91, 260[m]
4th	*12.1–10; 21.1*	Good Friday (extended)	133–148, 274	272–273[m]
5th	*13.1–2*	Easter	149–160, 324[n.23]	260[t]

Course #3: The Four Gospels: a Concern for Jews from Each

(4 sessions)

Session	Figures to Display	Subject Addressed	Pages to Assign in Advance from *Modern Jews Engage the New Testament*	
			Some Basic Material	Additional Preparation
1st	*15.1–5*	Mark on Judas the betrayer	176–191	40[b], 53[m], 123[m]
2nd	*16.1–10*	Matthew's "lost sheep of the house of Israel"	192–209	76[m], 82[t], 102[m]
3rd	*17.1–3*	Luke's myriads of Jews in early Christianity	210–218	270[b]–271[m]
4th	*18.1–2*	John's conspicuous use of "the Jews"	219–229	129[b], 245[m]

Course #4: How Christians Applied "Gospel Dynamics"

(8 sessions)

Session	Figures to Display	Subject Addressed	Pages to Assign in Advance from *Modern Jews Engage the New Testament*	
			Some Basic Material	Additional Preparation
1st	*8.1–5*	Introducing "Gospel Dynamics"	83-91, 273–274, 289^b–292^t, 352–354	75-82, 132, 159, 188–189, 208, 293^t, 297^t
2nd	*12.1–4* *13.1–2*	**AGGRANDIZEMENT** Jesus' Sanhedrin trial & burial	134^m–140^m, 142^b–144^t, 150^b–152	28^b, 125^b–126^t, 154^t, 157^m, 159^t, 314$^{n.9}$
3rd	*16.5* *16.6*	**ALLEGORIZING** Parables of Marriage Feast & Wicked Tenants	197^m–200^t, 317$^{n.31}$	200^m–202, 207^m, 208^b, 275^m
4th	*10.1–3* *15.3*	**INSERTING** Passover, betrayal announced	110–117, 274^m 181^m–183^t	
5th	*12.1–5,7–10;* *16.3; 21.1*	**INSERTING** (cont'd) Jesus' trial / blasphemy Barabbas / blood curse	126^b, 133–148, 195^b–196, 274, 322$^{n.10}$	51^m, 127^m, 129^m, 132^b, 143^b
6th	*8.2* *15.1–2* *16.4* *17.1–2*	**OMITTING** Jesus' last words, Judas, thrones, Shema / camaraderie, Institutions	86^m–88^m 179–181^m 196^b–197^t 212–213^m	206^m
7th	*Intro. Fig. 1–2* *6.2,5* *9.2–3*	**TYPOLOGY** Introduction Paul Infancy narratives	xiv–xvi, xx^b, 24^m, 82^m, 255^b–257^m, 354^m 61–62, 72, 175^m 97–98, 103^b–104^m, 106^m, 319$^{n.3}$, 320$^{n.14}$	
8th	*15.5* *13.1–2* *8.3; 11.1;* *12.2; 16.1*	**TYPOLOGY** (cont'd) Judas Joseph of Arimathea Jesus	177^m–178^t, 186, 327$^{n.21}$ 151^b 88^m–89^t, 106^m, 126^t, 127, 136^m–137^m, 193^b–194^t, 257^{tm}	

The
Figures
Presented

Preface

Customary Sequencing			Our Sequencing		
Text of Matthew ca. 85	Text of Mark ca. 72 (earliest Gospel)	Text of Luke ca. 94+	Text of Mark ca. 72 (earliest Gospel)	Text of Matthew ca. 85	Text of Luke ca. 94+

Preface Fig. 1—Resequencing Synoptic Columns

Introduction

Intro. Fig. 1 Synagoga

Justin Martyr (ca. 155)	Irenaeus (ca. 180)	Cyprian (ca. 250)
The marriages of Jacob were types .... **Leah** represented your people [the Jews] and the **Synagogue**; ... **Rachel** ... our **Church**.... As the eyes of **Leah** were weak, so too ... the eyes of your souls (*Dialogue with Trypho*, 134).	[Jacob] did all for the sake of the younger, **Rachel** ... type of the **Church**.... Christ was by his Patriarchs prefiguring ... things to come (*Against Heresies* IV, 21, 3).	Jacob received two wives: the elder, **Leah**, with weak eyes, a type of the **Synagogue**; the younger, the beautiful **Rachel**, a type of the **Church** (*Treatises* XII, 1, Testimony 20).

Intro. Fig. 2—Patristic Sources for Synagoga ("Synagogue") and Ecclesia ("Church")

Notes on Terminology

BODIES OF TEXT	LITERARY TERMS	THEOLOGY	SOCIAL CATEGORIES	GEOGRAPHY
Jewish Scripture	Synoptic	Christ/Messiah	Christians	Land of Israel
New Testament	Synoptist	The Word	Gentiles	Palestine
Tanakh	Synoptic Problem	Salvation/Saved	Gentile-Christians	Diaspora
Septuagint (LXX)	Evangelist	Apocalypse	Jewish-Christians	**CHRONOLOGY**
Canon/Apocrypha	Passion	Apocalyptists	Judaizers	BCE/CE
Rabbinic Literature	Passion Narrative	Eschatological	God-fearers	**SPECIAL**
(Midrash, Mishnah, Talmud)	Proof-texting	Son of Man	Pagans	Gospel Dynamics
	Typology	Son of God	Disciples/Apostles	
		Kerygma		

Term. Fig. 1—Order of Appearance of Terms within "Notes on Terminology"

Figures from Part One: Renouncing Intentional Ignorance

1.1— Basic Questions That Jews Find the Hardest to Answer

Theology (questions Christians ask Jews)	Holy Days (also, Christians ask Jews)	Enigma: Benefit vs. Blame (from Jews to themselves)
• Why won't you accept Jesus as the Jewish Messiah? • Isn't Jesus predicted in your own Bible? • Who *do* you think Jesus was? • Did not Jesus die for your sins? • Why not just accept Jesus and *remain* Jewish?	• *Christmas:* How do you account for Jesus' Virgin Birth? • *Maundy (Holy) Thursday:* Why won't you even attend our church Seder? • *Good Friday:* Why did you Jews kill Jesus? • *Easter:* How do you account for Jesus' empty tomb?	• If Christians say it was indispensable for humanity's salvation that Jesus die, and if Jews are said to be so vital a cog in effecting that "benefit," why are Jews *blamed* rather than *praised* for their (presumed) role in humanity's salvation?

1.2—Schneider-Shapiro's Questionnaire to Jewish Professionals

1. Does the figure of Jesus occupy any ... part of your education program?

2. If No, why not?
   - Opposition/Resistance from: Rabbi __, educator __, teachers __, parents __, children __ ...?
   - Never been implemented before and hard to introduce now? __
   - Rabbi/educator/teachers are not learned enough ... to ... implement ... such a program? __
   - No curricular materials available? __
   - Not enough time as is to teach about standard Jewish subjects? __ ...

3. If Yes, ...
   a. In what educational setting...?
   b. What is taught...?
   c. In what context...? (... study of Christianity? Comparative religion? Jewish historical development—if so, what ... period?)
   d. How long has this ... been in place?
   e. What brought about ... [its] implementation? (... requests from parents or students, intermarriage, converts, ... respond to ... Missionaries, ... personal interest by rabbi/educator/teacher?)
   f. How was the curriculum designed? ...
   g. How did the ... teacher prepare ... for teaching this material? ...
   h. What is the ... reaction ... [students, parents, education board, Temple board], etc.?

4. Conceptually or philosophically, why do you teach/not teach about Jesus? ...

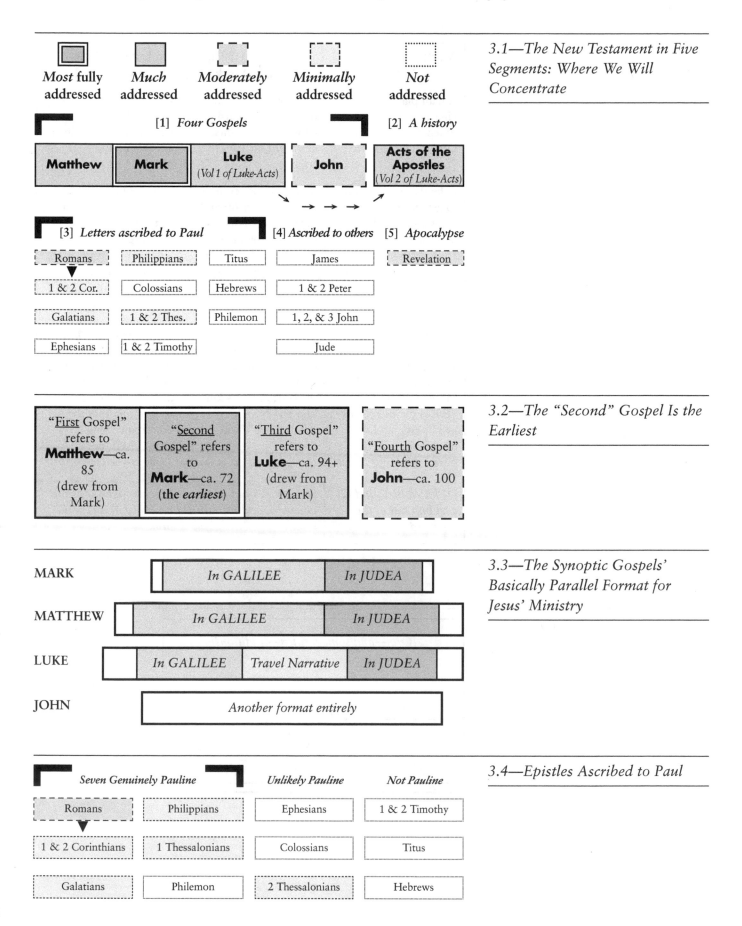

3.1—The New Testament in Five Segments: Where We Will Concentrate

Most fully addressed / Much addressed / Moderately addressed / Minimally addressed / Not addressed

[1] *Four Gospels*

Matthew — Mark — Luke (Vol 1 of Luke-Acts)

[2] *A history*

John — Acts of the Apostles (Vol 2 of Luke-Acts)

[3] *Letters ascribed to Paul*

Romans — Philippians — Titus
1 & 2 Cor. — Colossians — Hebrews
Galatians — 1 & 2 Thes. — Philemon
Ephesians — 1 & 2 Timothy

[4] *Ascribed to others*

James
1 & 2 Peter
1, 2, & 3 John
Jude

[5] *Apocalypse*

Revelation

3.2—The "Second" Gospel Is the Earliest

"First Gospel" refers to **Matthew**—ca. 85 (drew from Mark)

"Second Gospel" refers to **Mark**—ca. 72 (the *earliest*)

"Third Gospel" refers to **Luke**—ca. 94+ (drew from Mark)

"Fourth Gospel" refers to **John**—ca. 100

3.3—The Synoptic Gospels' Basically Parallel Format for Jesus' Ministry

MARK — In GALILEE | In JUDEA

MATTHEW — In GALILEE | In JUDEA

LUKE — In GALILEE | Travel Narrative | In JUDEA

JOHN — Another format entirely

3.4—Epistles Ascribed to Paul

Seven Genuinely Pauline | *Unlikely Pauline* | *Not Pauline*

Romans — Philippians — Ephesians — 1 & 2 Timothy
1 & 2 Corinthians — 1 Thessalonians — Colossians — Titus
Galatians — Philemon — 2 Thessalonians — Hebrews

3.5—Parable of the Wicked Tenants

Mark 12:1ff. (ca. 72) ▼	Matthew 21:33ff.— revises Mark	Luke 20:9ff.— revises Mark
A man planted a vineyard, ... let it out to tenants, and went into another country.	... a householder ... planted a vineyard ... let it out to tenants, and went into another country.	A man planted a vineyard, ... let it out to tenants, and went into another country ....
... he sent a servant ... to get from them some ... fruit of the vineyard .... They ... beat him .... He sent another ... and ... many others, some they beat and some they killed.	... he sent his servants ... to get his fruit; and the tenants ... beat one, killed another, and stoned another .... He sent other servants ... and they did the same to them.	... he sent a servant ... that they ... give him some of the fruit of the vineyard; but the tenants beat him .... He sent another ...; him also they beat .... And he sent yet a third ....
He had ... a beloved son; ... he sent him ..., saying, "they will respect my son." But those tenants said ..., "this is the heir; ... let us kill him, and the inheritance will be ours." And they ...	... he sent his son ..., saying, "they will respect my son." ... but ... they said ..., "this is the heir; ... let us kill him and have his inheritance." And they ...	... the owner ... said, ... "I will send my beloved son; ... they will respect him." But ... they said ..., "this is the heir; let us kill him, that the inheritance may be ours." And they ...
[1] killed him, and [2] cast him out of the vineyard.	*[2] cast him out of the vineyard, and [1] killed him.*	*[2] cast him out of the vineyard and [1] killed him.*

3.6—Matthew and Luke Draw on Mark

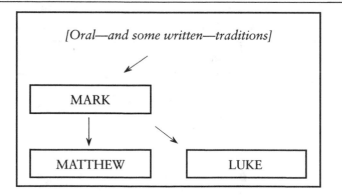

Mark	Matthew 6:9ff. ▼	Luke 11:2ff.
No Equivalent	Pray then like this: Our Father who art in heaven, hallowed be thy name. Thy kingdom come. Thy will be done, on earth as it is in heaven. Give us this day our daily bread; and forgive us our debts, as we also have forgiven our debtors; and lead us not into temptation, but deliver us from evil.	When you pray, say: Father, hallowed be thy name. Thy kingdom come. Give us each day our daily bread; and forgive us our sins, for we ourselves forgive every one who is indebted to us; and lead us not into temptation.

3.7—Sample of Matter Assigned to "Q"

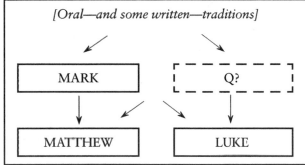

3.8—Matthew and Luke Draw on Another Shared Source Besides Mark

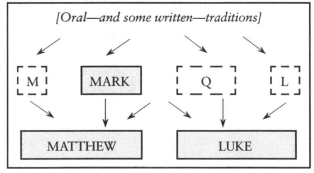

3.9—Four-Document Source Theory

Mark 14:43ff. ▼	Matthew 26:47ff.— revises Mark	Luke 22:47ff.— revises Mark
Judas came ... and with him a crowd with swords and clubs....	Judas came ... and with him a > **great** crowd with swords and clubs	there came a crowd, ... the man ... Judas ... leading them
And they laid hands on him and seized [Jesus]	Then they ... laid hands on Jesus and seized him	.... Then they seized [Jesus] ....
And all forsook him, and fled.	*All the disciples forsook him and fled*	*|> (CANCELS FLIGHT)*

3.10—Free Improvisation (i.e., Unaided by Sources)

Figures from Part Two: Basics We Should Know

4.1—*Christianity's Emergence*

	In the Land of ISRAEL			In the DIASPORA	
	Beginning with Jewish-Christians*			Beginning with Jewish-Christians and Gentile-Christians*	
Early 30s	Enclaves proliferate (with some elements filtering into the Diaspora)		Early 30s	After persecuting Damascus Christians, Paul joins them in accepting Jesus as the Christ; he commences missionary endeavors	
			50s	Paul's EPISTLES	
62	Execution of James		64?	Paul dies (in Rome?)	
66	Jerusalem church disappears				
70	Rome destroys 2nd Temple		72?	"MARK" (written in Rome?)	
			85?	"MATTHEW" (in Antioch?)	
			94–125?	"LUKE"-ACTS (in Greece?)	
			100?	"JOHN" (in Ephesus?)	
132–135	Bar Kokhba Revolt				
?			ca. 170	New Testament is coalescing	

4.2—*Two Basic Configurations*

"Configuration A" Christianity (beginning as a *Jesus* Movement)

Arose in the land of Israel—an outgrowth of a small number of Jews remaining impacted by, and committed to, teachings of Jesus, to their companionship, interactions, and exchanges with him, and to their consequent belief that he was the Messiah. They admitted that he did not conform to the then political expectations for this figure, and at first were demoralized by his crucifixion. But they rebounded through faith that he rose from the dead and would imminently return to complete his mission. Some cadres of this **Jesus Movement** spread into the Diaspora, enduring longer in some areas than others. But fading, Configuration A exerted little impact on the Christianity that endured.

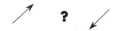

"Configuration B" Christianity (becoming a *Paul* Movement)

Arose primarily in the Diaspora—integrating its early beliefs with antecedent Greco-Roman religious currents that served as a matrix-in-waiting, absorbing and mutating the Jesus figure into a *cosmic Lord*. This Configuration attracted Paul. He deepened it by incorporating motifs derivative from his Judaism (especially atoning sacrifice, or atonement through sacrifice), and sacramental benefits akin to those promised by Mystery cults of dying and rising savior deities (to be detailed later in this chapter). This **Paul Movement** became the nucleus of a Christianity that endured.

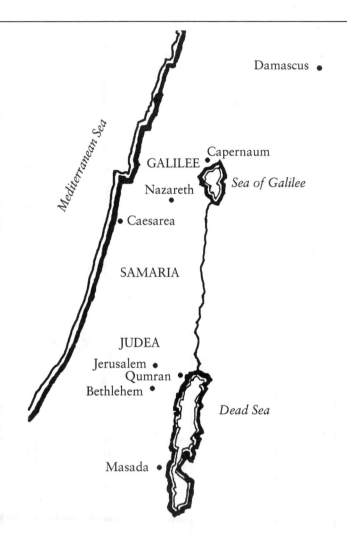

5.2—Highlights of the Period of the Second Temple in Judea

A	B	C	D			E				
			INSTITUTIONS			GROUPINGS				
Dates	Ruling Power	Local Ruler				1	2	3	4	5
586–538	Babylonian Exile		S E C O N D T E M P L E	S A N H E D R I N	S Y N A G O G U E	P H A R I S E E S / Scribes	Priesthood / S A D D U C E E S	Qumran / Essenes	A C T I V I S T S	C H R I S T I A N S
538–333	Persian Rule									
333–142	Greek Rule									
142–63	Independence	Hasmoneans								
63–	Roman Rule									
37–4		Herod								
4		Archelaus ▼	▼	▼	▼					
- - - -	- 0 -									
6		# 1								
		# 2								
		# 3								
		# 4								
		# 5								
		# 6					▼			
		# 7						▼		
41–44		Agrippa I								
		# 8				▼			▼	
		# 9								
		# 10								
		# 11								
		# 12								
		# 13								
66		# 14								
70				▼		▼				▼
80		Gamaliel II		Sanhedrin reconstituted		Rabbis				
132–135		Bar Kokhba								

POLITICALLY Conceived		TRANSCENDENTALLY Conceived
	Most ▼	
The **arena** conceived is *this-*worldly: God assumes rule over Rome *without* the present order dissolved	⟷	The **arena** conceived is *next-*worldly: God assumes rule *with* the present order dissolved
	⟷	
The **scope of concerns** is *exclusivistic nationalism* aiming to secure Israel's independence and power	⟷	The **scope of concerns** is *universalistic*: Gentiles also are beneficiaries of God's plan
The **world to come** betokens *material* prosperity and bliss *on earth* (at least in Israel)	⟷	The **world to come** emphasizes *spiritual* ascendancy and bliss *in heaven*
The **antagonists**: *Israel vs. Rome*	⟷	The **antagonists**: *God vs. supernatural powers of evil* (Satan and his hosts)
The **Messiah**: an earthly *human* temporal ruler in Israel (likely a Davidic descendant); he will annihilate Israel's enemies or proclaim God's doing so imminently	⟷	The **Messiah**: a transcendent (heavenly, even preexistent) being, recalling Daniel 7:13's "Son of man"*

5.3—A Continuum of the Apocalyptic Mind-set

Tier I Emperor	Tiberius / 14–37	Caligula, 37–41; Claudius, 41–54; Nero, 54–68
Tier II Roman Governor	Pilate / 26–37	9 more Governors before the Great Revolt, in 66
Tier III High Priest	Caiaphas / 18–37	15 more High Priests before the Temple's fall, in 70

5.4—Three Tiers of Authority in Judea (Inclusive of the Period 30–66)

5.5—A Conceptualization of Judea in Jesus' Day

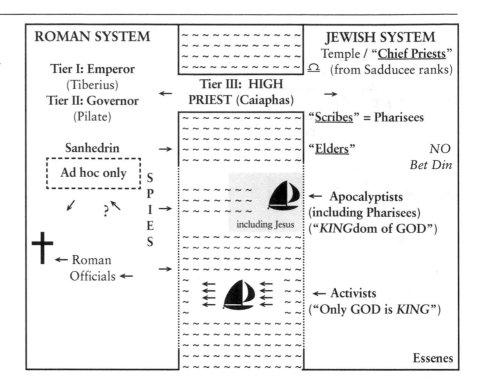

5.6—The Temple's Fall as a Watershed for Jews

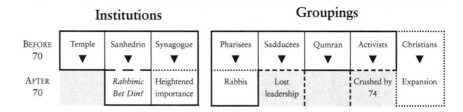

	Institutions			Groupings				
	Temple	Sanhedrin	Synagogue	Pharisees	Sadducees	Qumran	Activists	Christians
BEFORE 70	▼	▼	▼	▼	▼	▼	▼	▼
AFTER 70		*Rabbinic Bet Din?*	Heightened importance	Rabbis	Lost leadership		Crushed by 74	Expansion

Mk 15:37ff.	Jesus ... breathed his last. And the curtain of the temple was torn in two.
	[Comment: This curtain was penetrated by the high priest solely on the Day of Atonement (Yom Kippur) so he could effect expiation for the sins of the people. Now Jesus' expiration effected this atonement, for all time ending any need for the Temple, not to mention for the curtain.]
Mt 27:24f.	Pilate ... washed his hands ... saying, "I am innocent of this man's blood...." And all the people answered, "His blood be on us and on our children!"
	[Comment: This is Matthew's theological justification, in the 80s, for the Temple's fall in 70.]
I Thes 2:13ff.	The Jews ... killed ... the Lord Jesus.... God's wrath has come upon them at last!
	[Comment: The "wrath" refers to the Temple's fall. I consider this passage added by a post-Pauline hand— see Chap. 11.]
Heb 9:11ff.	Christ ... entered once for all ... into the Holy Place, taking not ... blood of goats and calves but his own blood ... securing an eternal redemption.
	[Comment: As both perfect high priest and perfect sacrifice, Christ replaces the Temple.]

5.7—How Christian Theology Processed the Temple's Fall

Mk 11:15 & parr	He ... began to drive out those who sold and ... bought in the **temple**, and he overturned the tables of the money-changers....
Mk 13:1ff. & parr	As he came out of the **temple**, one of his disciples said..., "Look ... what wonderful ... buildings!" ... Jesus said ... " ... There will not be left ... one stone upon another ... not ... thrown down."
Mk 14:57f. & par	Some ... bore *false* witness..., "We heard him say, 'I will destroy this **temple** ... made with hands, and in three days ... build another, not made with hands.'"
Mk 15:29 & par	Those who passed by derided him, wagging their heads ..., "... You who would destroy the **temple** and build it in three days, save yourself ... come down from the cross!"
Jn 2:19ff.	"Destroy this **temple**, and in three days I will raise it up." ... But he spoke of the **temple** of his body.

5.8—Frequent Surfacings of the Temple Accusation

6.1—Paul's Before-and-After Testimony Concerning Persecution

- **Concerning Paul as Persecutor (*Pre*-"Conversion")**

  Gal 1:13 — You have heard of my former life in Judaism, how I *persecuted the church ... violently and tried to destroy it.*

  1 Cor 15:9 — I am ... unfit to be called an apostle, because *I persecuted the church.*

  Gal 1:22f. — ... the churches ... in Judea only heard ... "He who once *persecuted* us is now preaching the faith he *once tried to destroy.*"

  Phil 3:6 — As to zeal [I had been] a *persecutor of the church.*

- **Concerning Paul as Persecuted (*Post*-"Conversion")**

  2 Cor 11:23ff. — Are [my rival apostles; cf. verse 5] servants of Christ? I am ... better.... *Five times I ... received at the hands of the Jews ... forty lashes less one. Three times ... beaten with rods; once ... stoned.*

  Rom 15:30f. — Pray ... that I may be *delivered from the unbelievers in Judea.*

6.2—Acts' "Damascus Road" Drama Echoes Ezekiel's Vision

Ezek 1:28; 2:1ff.—the brightness ... was the appearance of the likeness of the glory of the Lord.... When I saw it, I fell upon my face, and I heard the voice ... speaking ... "... I send you to the people of **Israel.**"

Acts 22:6ff.,21—As I ... drew near to Damascus ... a great light from heaven ... shone about me.... I fell to the ground and heard a voice.... "Depart; for I ... send you ... to the **Gentiles.**"

Gal 1:15f.	When he ... was pleased to **reveal** his Son to me....
1 Cor 9:1ff.	Am I not an apostle? Have I not **seen** Jesus our Lord?... You are the seal of my apostleship in the Lord. This is my defense to those who would examine me....
1 Cor 15:3ff.	I delivered to you ... what I also received,

> that Christ died for our sins ... was buried ... was raised on the third day ... and ... **appeared** to Cephas, then to the twelve. Then ... **appeared** to more than five hundred brethren.... Then ... **appeared** to James, then ... all the apostles.

Last of all, as to one untimely born, he **appeared** also to me.

6.3—The Three Key Pauline Verbs

Total uses of each term ↓								
Paradigm That Paul Uses	Total #	Rom	1 Cor	2 Cor	Gal	Phil	1 Thes	Phile
"Jesus" alone	*15*	*2*	*1*	*7*	*1*	*1*	*3*	*0*
"Christ" alone	160	33	44	39	21	17	3	3
"Lord" alone	107	19	44	18	2	9	13	2
Cosmic variants (below)	59	15	13	8	3	6	11	3
Total references	341	69	102	72	27	33	30	8

"Lord"[11] and "Christ" variants are very diverse: "Christ Jesus our Lord," "Christ Jesus my Lord," "Lord Jesus Christ," "Jesus Christ our Lord," "his Son, Jesus Christ our Lord," "Lord Christ," "the Lord Jesus," "Jesus Christ as Lord," "Jesus Christ is Lord," "Jesus our Lord," and "Jesus is Lord."

6.4—Paul's Rare Use of "Jesus" Alone, versus Cosmic Terms

Isaiah's Call	Jeremiah's Call	Paul's Call
Isa 49:1ff.—The Lord called me *from the womb....*	*Jer 1:4ff.*—The word of the Lord: ... **"Before I formed you in the womb ... and before you were born** ... I appointed you a prophet **to the nations** [Gentiles]."	*Gal 1:11ff.*—When he who had **set me apart before I was born,** and ... called me ... was pleased to **reveal** his Son to me ... that *I* **might preach him among ... Gentiles....**
" ... I ... give you as a light *to the nations* [Gentiles].... "		

6.5—Paul Expresses His Call to Gentiles in Isaiah's and Jeremiah's Terms

Figures from Part Three: Reasoning Matters Through

8.1—Twenty Sample Problems Confronting Early Christians (That Gospels Could Be Addressing)

	Problems INTERNAL to Early Christian Communities
	• Discomfort over perceptions that Jesus had died a victim, not a victor
	• Pressure to redefine "Messiah" in view of Jesus' crucifixion
	• Impatience / frustration / doubt over delay in the Second Coming
	• Urgency to stem defections from Christian ranks
	• Anxiety over betrayals of Christians to Rome (by trusted companions, even relatives)
	• Divisiveness generated by rifts over ritual practice

		Problems EXTERNAL to Early Christian Communities—Posed by Others
Rome		• How to stem Roman persecution of Christians (commencing during the 60s)
		• How to disassociate Christians (in Roman eyes) from the image of Jewish rebels (66–73)
		• How to explain that Jesus' crucifixion did not mean that his later followers were seditionists
		• How to shift blame for Jesus' death from Rome to another party (here, the Jews)
		• How to convey that Jesus was condemned only for "blasphemy" (of no concern to Rome)
Jews		• How to demonstrate that Elijah—herald of the Messiah—already had appeared
		• How to establish that Jesus was the Messiah despite his failure to fulfil Jewish expectations
		• How to show that Jewish scriptures predicted Jesus' coming
		• How to refine the concept of God's chosen people so as to include Gentile-Christians*
		• How to justify departures from the Law of Moses by Gentile-Christians
		• How to refute Jews' denials of Jesus' resurrection
		• How to cope with ejections of some Jewish-Christians* from the synagogue
Rivals	*The Baptist*	• How to compete with the rival John the Baptist movement
	Gnostics	• How to prove that the Christ genuinely took on flesh

Mark 15:34ff.	Matthew 27:46ff.	Luke 23:46	John 19:30
... Jesus cried with a loud voice ... *"My God, my God, why hast thou forsaken me?"* [Ps 22:1]....	... Jesus cried with a loud voice ... *"My God, my God, why hast thou forsaken me?"* [Ps 22:1]	[NO INITIAL CRY AT ALL]	he said, *"It is finished"*;
Jesus uttered a loud [WORDLESS] cry,	... Jesus cried again [WORDLESSLY] with a loud voice	Then Jesus, crying with a loud voice, said, *"Father, into thy hands I commit my spirit!"* [Ps 31:5]	[NO OTHER CRY]
and breathed his last.	and yielded up his spirit.	And ... he breathed his last.	and he ... gave up his spirit.

8.2—Were "Jesus' Last Words" Replaced?

Psalm 22 (BCE)		Mark 15 (ca. 72 CE)
1 My God, my God, why hast thou forsaken me?...	→	34 ... Jesus cried ... "My God, my God, why hast thou forsaken me?"
6 ... scorned by men, ... despised by the people. 7All ... mock at me ... wag their heads....	→	29 ... those who passed by derided him, wagging their heads....
16 ... evildoers encircle me; they have pierced my hands and feet....	→	24 And they crucified him,
18 they divide my garments among them, ... for my raiment they cast lots....	→	and divided his garments among them, casting lots for them....

8.3—Was the Crucifixion Scene Conformed to Psalm 22?

Mark 16:5ff.	Matthew 28:2ff. —revises Mark	Luke 24:4ff. —revises Mark
a young man ... said ..., "... Jesus ... has risen ... go ... go, tell his disciples and Peter that	an *angel* ... said ..., "... Jesus... has risen ... go ... tell his disciples that ...	*two men* ... said ..., "Why do you seek the living among the dead?
he is going before you *to Galilee*; there you will see him, as *he* told you."	he is going before you *to Galilee*; there you will see him. Lo, *I have told you*."	Remember how *he* told you, *while he was still in Galilee*, that...."

8.4—Luke Prevents Jesus' Followers from Leaving Judea

8.5—*Did Mark Expand the Passion in Anti-Jewish Ways?*	*Pre-Marcan*	*After Mark's Expansion*

Essentially neutral toward Jews

← ← **THE SANHEDRIN TRIAL?** ← ← *Anti-Jewish*

Essentially neutral toward Jews

← ← **THE BARABBAS EPISODE?** ← ← *Anti-Jewish*

Essentially neutral toward Jews

Figures from Part Four: Christian Holy Days: Beneficial Applications of Jewish Gospel Study

AS THE FIRST CENTURY ADVANCES—*earlier* writers to *later*— THE MOMENT WHEN CHRIST-JESUS' DIVINITY IS EVINCED REGRESSES—*later to earlier*				
	(1)	(2)	(3)	(4)
At the time of ➤	Paul's epistles	Mark	**Matthew and Luke**	John
datable around ➤	the 50s	72	**the 80s–90s**	100
the moment when Christ-Jesus' divinity is made manifest to the reader is ➤	Jesus' resurrection	Jesus' (adult) baptism	**Jesus' (virginal) conception**	Christ's pre-existence

9.1—The Regressive Shift of the "Moment of Manifestation"

- Jesus' genealogy through Joseph's *male* line.
- Mary and Joseph **LIVE IN BETHLEHEM**.
- During her betrothal, Mary is found with child.
- An angel reassures a suspicious Joseph in a dream.
- Jesus is born in Bethlehem.
- Having seen a STAR, MAGI come to **JERUSALEM**,
- Then follow the STAR to **BETHLEHEM**.
- King Herod poses a danger to Jesus.
- Joseph's second dream alerts the family to flee to **EGYPT**.
- Herod dies.
- A third dream prompts the family to return from Egypt.
- A fourth dream detours them northward, to **NAZARETH**.

9.2—Matthew's Infancy Narrative (ca. 85)

- Gabriel promises Zechariah John the Baptist's birth;
- Elizabeth conceives.
- Gabriel makes his annunciation to Mary in **NAZARETH**.
- Mary visits Elizabeth (at length); then returns to Nazareth.
- John the Baptist is born.
- Mary approaches term *in* **NAZARETH**.
- Joseph and Mary go *to* **BETHLEHEM** for a census.
- With no room in the inn, Jesus is born in a manger.
- ANGELS and SHEPHERDS appear.
- Jesus is circumcised.
- Jesus is presented in the Temple in **JERUSALEM**.
- The holy family leave Jerusalem to *return* to **NAZARETH**.

9.3—Luke's Infancy Narrative (ca. 95)

9.4—Disparities Between Infancy Narratives in Matthew and Luke

MATTHEW	← →	LUKE
Perilous	Ambience?	Tranquil
To Joseph	The angel announces to whom?	To Mary
In Bethlehem	Where?	In Nazareth
She resides there	Mary delivers in Bethlehem because ...	She travels there
None needed	Is an inn sought?	Yes
No	Angels and shepherds?	Yes
Yes	Magi and the Star?	No
Yes	Holy family flees to Egypt?	No
Yes	Herod massacres Bethlehem infants?	No
No	Jesus' circumcision noted?	Yes
No	Jesus' first-born redemption ceremony?	Yes
No	John the Baptist's birth story?	Yes
No	The boy Jesus (at 12) engages sages?	Yes
Yes	Is a genealogy tied to the story?	No

9.5—The Christmas Composite

Gabriel promises Zechariah John the Baptist's birth; Elizabeth conceives. In NAZARETH, Gabriel reveals to Mary what her special role will be. After visiting Elizabeth in *Judea*, Mary returns to Nazareth in *Galilee*. John the Baptist is born.

Luke 1

▼

During betrothal, Mary finds herself with child. Joseph is disposed to divorce her but an angel reassures him (in a dream) that Mary has conceived through the Holy Spirit, not another man.

Matthew 1

Despite Mary's advanced pregnancy, Joseph takes her to BETHLEHEM to register in a census. With no room in the inn, Jesus is born in a manger. Angels and shepherds appear. After circumcision, Jesus is brought to JERUSALEM's Temple for a first-born's redemption ceremony.

Luke 2

☆ *Invented Segue—the Family's Return to Bethlehem from Jerusalem*

Magi, having seen a star in the east, arrive in Jerusalem. Upon learning there where Jesus has been born, they travel to BETHLEHEM, with the star guiding them. After adoring the infant, they return eastward to their home. Joseph dreams that he, Mary, and Jesus must flee to EGYPT from Herod, who soon after massacres all of Bethlehem's male infants. Once Herod dies, the holy family return from Egypt and settle in NAZARETH.

Matthew 2

10.1—Was the Last Supper a Passover Meal?

ORDINARY MEAL	*1 Cor 11:23 (mid-50s)*—In Paul's sole reference to the Last Supper ("the Lord Jesus, on the night when he was delivered up [to death], took bread"), the Greek word Paul uses is that for regular bread (*artos*), not the proper designation for unleavened bread (*azyma*), and Paul conveys no awareness that this meal might have been a Passover observance.
PASSOVER MEAL	*Mark (ca. 72)*—Here the entire case for identifying the Last Supper as a Passover meal rests with a single, five-verse paragraph (14:12–16).
(Ambiguous)	*Matthew (ca. 85)* and *Luke* (ca. 95)—Finding Mark's account problematic, both Matthew and Luke replicate Mark's general scheme, yet refine it in ways that, to us, may appear to undermine Mark's credibility.
ORDINARY MEAL	*John (ca. 100)*—John presents the Last Supper as occurring twenty-four hours→ *before* the Passover meal.

1–2:	It was now two days *before* the Passover and the Feast of Unleavened Bread. And the chief priests and ... scribes were seeking how to arrest him ... and kill him; for they said, "*Not during the feast*, lest there be a tumult of the people." ...
10–11:	Then Judas Iscariot ... went to the chief priests ... to betray him to them ... and he sought an opportunity....

And *on the first day of Unleavened Bread*, when they sacrificed the Passover Lamb, his disciples said to him, "Where will you have us ... prepare for you to eat the Passover?" And he sent *two* of his disciples: ... "*Go into the city*, and a man carrying a jar of water will meet you; ... wherever he enters, say to the householder, 'The Teacher says, "Where is my guest room, where I am to eat the Passover with my disciples?"' And he will show you a large upper room furnished and ready; there prepare for us." And the disciples ... *went to the city* and found it as he had told them; and they prepared the Passover.

Passover meal created and inserted belatedly

17–20:	... When it was evening he *came with the twelve*. And as they were at table eating, Jesus said, "... one of you will betray me, one ... dipping *bread* in the same dish with me...."
22–25:	... as they were eating, he took *bread*, ... blessed ... broke it, and gave it to them.... "Take; this is my body." ... He took a cup, and ... gave it to them, and they all drank.... He said..., "This is my blood of the covenant ... poured out for many...."
26:	And ... they went out to the Mount of Olives.

10.2—Mark's Insertion of His Invented "Passover" Paragraph

Mark 14:17	Matthew 26:20	Luke 22:14
And when it was evening he came with the twelve	When it was evening, he *sat at table* with the twelve disciples	And when the *hour* came, he *sat at table*, and the apostles with him

10.3—Matthew and Luke Believe Mark Has Made an Error

11.1—Parallels Between Jeremiah and Jesus

Jeremiah		Jesus
"Has the house ... become a den of robbers ...?" (7:11)	→	"Is it not written [Jer 7:11], 'My house ... you have made ... a den of robbers'?" (Mk 11:17 & parr)
I will "do to th[is] house [temple #1] ... as I did to Shiloh [1 Sa 4–6]!" (7:14)	→	"We heard him say, 'I will destroy this temple [#2] ...'" (Mk 14:58 & par; cf. Jn 2:19)
"All the people laid hold of him, saying: 'You shall die'" (26:8)	→	"All the people" demanded his death (Mt 27:25)
An inquiry convened for Jeremiah (26:10)	→	A Sanhedrin convened for Jesus (Mk 14:53 & parr)
Priests (and others) said Jeremiah "deserves ... death" for words that "you have heard" (26:11)	→	The Sanhedrin decided that Jesus "deserves death" (Mt 26:66 [cf. Mk 14:64]) for words that "you have heard" (Mk 14:64; cf. Mt 26:65)
"you will bring innocent blood upon yourselves" (26:15)	→	"His blood be on us and on our children!" (Mt 27:25)
His captors took him for execution to the vacillating King Zedekiah, who replied: "He is in your hands ..." (38:5)	→	His captors took him for execution to the vacillating prefect Pilate, who replied: "See to it yourselves" (Mt 27:24)
Wanting a private conversation, "Zedekiah sent for Jeremiah" (38:14)	→	Wanting a private conversation, "Pilate ... called Jesus" to him (Jn 18:33)
Zedekiah was "afraid" (38:19)	→	Pilate was "the more afraid" (Jn 19:8)

11.2—The "Hybrid Riddle"

Benefit		Blame
If it was indispensable for the world's redemption that Jesus die, and if the Jews were a vital cog in effecting that "benefit,"	→	then why "blame" the Jews for Jesus' death rather than praising them for their key role in effecting it?

The SANHEDRIN Trial and Adjoining Materials					The BARABBAS Episode and Context		
14:53	14:54	14:55–65	14:66–72	15:1	15:2–5	15:6–15a	15:15b
Jesus *delivered* to HIGH PRIEST	Peter denies Jesus	√ SANHEDRIN Trial →	Peter denies Jesus (cont'd)	Jesus *delivered* to PILATE	PILATE interrogates Jesus	√ BARABBAS Episode	PILATE consigns Jesus to cross

12.1—The Most Anti-Jewish Components of Mark's Passion (14:53–15:15)

12.2—The Sanhedrin Mosaic of Five Accruing Layers

A 55 Now the chief priests and the whole council [Sanhedrin] sought testimony against Jesus to put him to death; but they found none. 56 For many *bore false witness against him*, and *their witness did not agree.*

B 57 And some stood up and *bore false witness against him*, saying, 58 "We heard him say, 'I will destroy this temple that is made with hands, and in three days I will build another, not made with hands.'" 59 Yet *not even so did their testimony agree.*

C 60 And the high priest [Caiaphas] stood up in the midst, and asked Jesus,

[Query #1] *"Have you no answer to make? What is it that these men testify against you?"* 61 But he was *silent* and made no answer.

Again the high priest asked him,

[Query #2] *"Are you the Christ, the Son of the Blessed?"* 62 And Jesus said, "I am; and you will see the Son of man seated at the right hand of Power, and coming with the clouds of heaven."

D 63 And the high priest tore his garments, and said, "Why do we still need witnesses? 64 You have heard his *blasphemy*. What is your decision?" And they *all* condemned him as deserving death.

E 65 And some began to spit on him, and to cover his face, and to strike him, saying to him, "Prophesy!" And the guards received him with blows.

12.3—Mark Inserts the Sanhedrin Trial Between the "Delivery" Texts (Short Form)

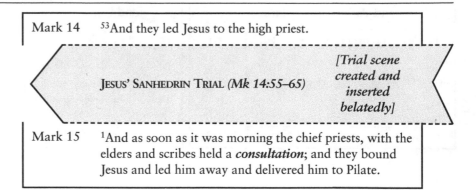

Mark 14   ⁵³And they led Jesus to the high priest.

JESUS' SANHEDRIN TRIAL *(Mk 14:55–65)*   *[Trial scene created and inserted belatedly]*

Mark 15   ¹And as soon as it was morning the chief priests, with the elders and scribes held a *consultation*; and they bound Jesus and led him away and delivered him to Pilate.

12.4—Mark's Editorial Fingerprints (Shaded)

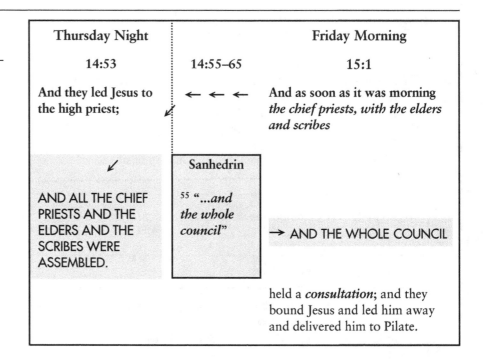

Thursday Night		**Friday Morning**
14:53	**14:55–65**	**15:1**
And they led Jesus to the high priest;	← ← ←	And as soon as it was morning *the chief priests, with the elders and scribes*
AND ALL THE CHIEF PRIESTS AND THE ELDERS AND THE SCRIBES WERE ASSEMBLED.	Sanhedrin ⁵⁵ "...*and the whole council*"	→ AND THE WHOLE COUNCIL
		held a *consultation*; and they bound Jesus and led him away and delivered him to Pilate.

12.5—What Remains as the "Residue" from 14:53–15:15 shaded—Marcan expansions white backdrop—"residue"

14:53	14:54	14:55–65	14:66–72	15:1	15:2–5	15:6–15a	15:15b
Jesus delivered to HIGH PRIEST	PETER denies Jesus	SANHEDRIN A B C *Query #1* *Query #2* D *Blasphemy* E →	PETER denies Jesus	Jesus delivered to PILATE	PILATE interrogates Jesus *Query #1* *Query #2*	BARABBAS *"King of the Jews"* ↵ *"King of the Jews"*	PILATE consigns Jesus to cross

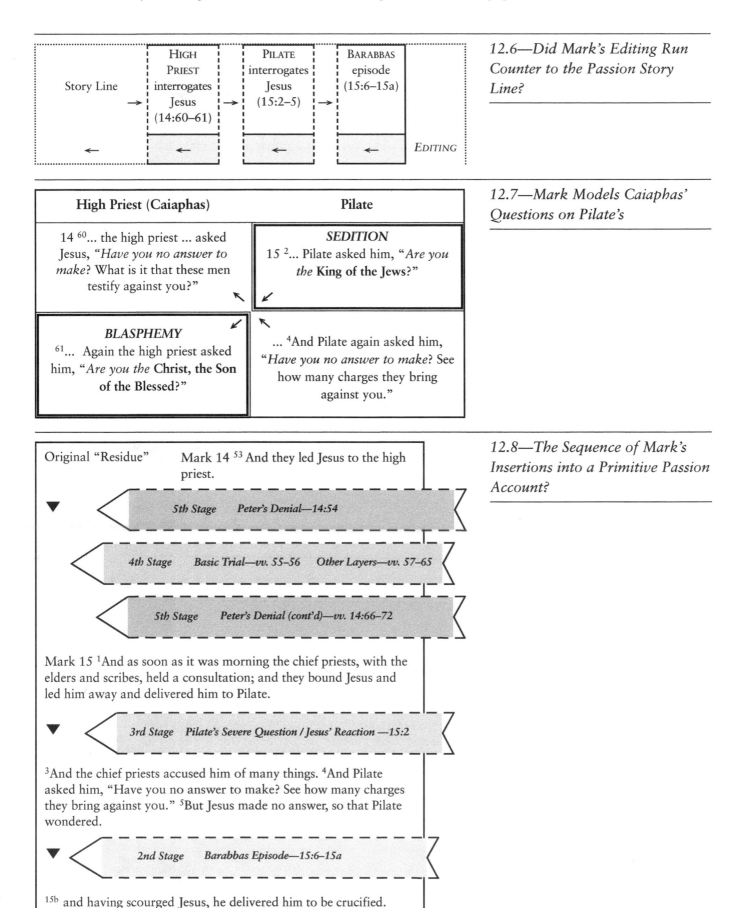

12.6—Did Mark's Editing Run Counter to the Passion Story Line?

Story Line	→	High Priest interrogates Jesus (14:60–61)	→	Pilate interrogates Jesus (15:2–5)	→	Barabbas episode (15:6–15a)
←		←		←		←	Editing

12.7—Mark Models Caiaphas' Questions on Pilate's

High Priest (Caiaphas)	**Pilate**
14 60... the high priest ... asked Jesus, "*Have you no answer to make*? What is it that these men testify against you?"	***SEDITION*** 15 2... Pilate asked him, "*Are you the* **King of the Jews**?"
BLASPHEMY 61... Again the high priest asked him, "*Are you the* **Christ, the Son of the Blessed**?"	... 4And Pilate again asked him, "*Have you no answer to make*? See how many charges they bring against you."

12.8—The Sequence of Mark's Insertions into a Primitive Passion Account?

Original "Residue"   Mark 14 53 And they led Jesus to the high priest.

▼ *5th Stage   Peter's Denial—14:54*

4th Stage   Basic Trial—vv. 55–56   Other Layers—vv. 57–65

5th Stage   Peter's Denial (cont'd)—vv. 14:66–72

Mark 15 1And as soon as it was morning the chief priests, with the elders and scribes, held a consultation; and they bound Jesus and led him away and delivered him to Pilate.

▼ *3rd Stage   Pilate's Severe Question / Jesus' Reaction —15:2*

3And the chief priests accused him of many things. 4And Pilate asked him, "Have you no answer to make? See how many charges they bring against you." 5But Jesus made no answer, so that Pilate wondered.

▼ *2nd Stage   Barabbas Episode—15:6–15a*

15b and having scourged Jesus, he delivered him to be crucified.

12.9—Mark Foreshadows the Sanhedrin Verdict

First, Mark plans the Sanhedrin verdict (chapter 14)

| 1 | 2 | 3 | 4 | 5 | 6 | 7 | 8 | 9 | 10 | 11 | 12 | 13 | 14 | 15 | 16 |

Second, Mark foreshadows the Sanhedrin verdict (chapter 2)

12.10—Mark's Insertion Elongates the Paralytic's Healing

2 ¹ ...He returned to Capernaum ... [and] was reported ... at home.... ³... They came, bringing to him a paralytic.... ⁵ ... When Jesus saw their faith, *he said to the paralytic* [originally followed by verse 11],

"... Your sins are forgiven." ⁶... Some ... *scribes* ... questioned ... ⁷ "Why does this man speak thus? It is *blasphemy!* ..." ⁸... Jesus ... said ... ⁹ "Which is easier, to say ..., 'Your sins are forgiven,' or ... 'Rise, take up your pallet and walk'? ¹⁰ But that you may know that *the Son of man* has authority ... to forgive sins" — *he said to the paralytic*

[Blasphemy unit inserted belatedly]

¹¹ "*I say to you*, rise, take up your pallet and go home." ¹²And he ... took up the pallet and went....

13.1—Mark's Renditions of the Burial and Empty Tomb

FRIDAY AFTERNOON **Burial (15:42–47)**	**SUNDAY MORNING** **Empty Tomb (16:1–8)**
Joseph of Arimathea, a respected member of the council [or "an honorable councilor"], ... also himself looking for the kingdom of God, took courage and went to Pilate, and asked for the body of Jesus. ... When [Pilate] learned ... that [Jesus] was dead, he granted the body to Joseph ... [who] ... taking him down, wrapped him in the linen shroud, and laid him in a tomb ... hewn out of the rock; and ... rolled a stone against the door.... Mary Magdalene and Mary the mother of Joses saw where he was laid.	... When the sabbath was past, [on Saturday night] Mary Magdalene, and Mary the mother of James, and Salome, bought spices ... that they might go and anoint ... [Jesus' body].... They went to the tomb when the sun had risen [Sunday morning]. ... They were saying to one another, "Who will roll away the stone for us from the door of the tomb?" ... Looking up, they saw that the stone was rolled back—it was very large. ... Entering the tomb, they saw a young man ... dressed in a white robe.... He said..., "... You seek Jesus of Nazareth, who was crucified. He has risen, he is not here; see the place where they laid him. But go, tell his disciples and Peter that he is going before you to Galilee; there you will see him, as he told you." ... They went out and fled ... the tomb; for trembling and astonishment had come upon them; and *they said nothing to any one*, for they were afraid.

MK 15:42–47; MT 27:57–61; LK 23:50–56A; JN 19:38–42	
MARK says only that Joseph • was a RESPECTED COUNCILOR • who was LOOKING FOR the KINGDOM OF GOD • showed COURAGE in requesting Jesus' body • laid it in a TOMB • and CLOSED the entrance	MATTHEW adds that Joseph • was RICH and Jesus' DISCIPLE • and OWNED the NEW tomb that he HAD HEWN PERSONALLY LUKE adds that Joseph • was GOOD and RIGHTEOUS • NOT CONSENTING to the council's verdict • and the tomb was NEVER BEFORE USED JOHN adds that Joseph • was Jesus' disciple SECRETLY, • and was aided by NICODEMUS

13.2—A Breakdown of Joseph of Arimathea's Attributes

Figures from Part Five: Primary New Testament Writings: A Concern for Jews from Each

15.1 — *The Synoptists' Concern to Pare "Twelve" to "Eleven"*

Mk	16:14	Afterward, he appeared to the *eleven*
Mt	28:16	The *eleven* disciples went to Galilee
Lk	24:9	Returning from the tomb they told all this to the *eleven*
	24:33	They found the *eleven* gathered together
Acts	1:13	They went up to the upper room ... [1] Peter and [2] John and [3] James and [4] Andrew, [5] Philip and [6] Thomas, [7] Bartholomew and [8] Matthew, [9] James ... and [10] Simon ... and [11] Judas the son of James [a Judas different from Iscariot]
	1:26	Matthias ... was enrolled with the *eleven* apostles*

15.2—*Luke's Omission of the Number of Thrones*

Matthew 19:28	**Luke 22:28ff.**
... in the new world ... you who have followed me will ... sit on *twelve* thrones, judging the *twelve* tribes of Israel....	*You* are those who have continued with me ... I appoint for *you*, that *you* may ... in my kingdom ... sit on _____ thrones judging the *twelve* tribes of Israel.

15.3—*Was Jesus' Prediction of the Betrayal Spliced into Mark 14?*

EARLY Version?	**Prediction ADDED?**	**SPLICED Text?**
[17]... he came with the twelve.		[17]... he came with the twelve.
↕	[18]**And as they were at table eating**, Jesus said ... " ... one of you will betray me...." ⟶	[18]**And as they were at table eating**, Jesus said ... " ... one of you will betray me...."
[22]**And as they were eating**, he took bread.		[22]**And as they were eating**, he took bread.

15.4—*The Pattern of Delivering Up in Mark*

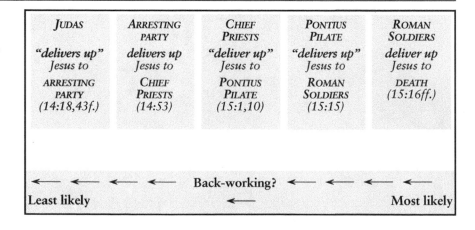

JUDAS	*ARRESTING PARTY*	*CHIEF PRIESTS*	*PONTIUS PILATE*	*ROMAN SOLDIERS*
"delivers up" Jesus to	*delivers up* Jesus to	*"deliver up"* Jesus to	*"delivers up"* Jesus to	*deliver up* Jesus to
ARRESTING PARTY (14:18,43f.)	*CHIEF PRIESTS (14:53)*	*PONTIUS PILATE (15:1,10)*	*ROMAN SOLDIERS (15:15)*	*DEATH (15:16ff.)*

← ← ← ← Back-working? ← ← ← ←
Least likely ← **Most likely**

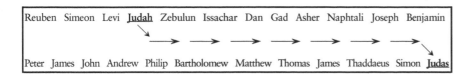

15.5—*The Influence of the Joseph Story on Selecting the Traitor's Name?*

Jesus (in Matthew)		Moses (in the Torah)		Commonalities
Chaps	1 & 2	Exod	1:1–2:10	Infancy narrative
Chap	3:13–17	Exod	14:10–31	Crossing water
Chap	4:1–11	Exod	16:1–17:7	Wilderness temptation
Chaps	5, 6, & 7	Exod	19:1–23:23	Law-giving from a mountain
Chap	17:1–9	Exod	34:29–35	Transfiguration atop a mountain
Chap	28:16–20	Deut	31:7–9 (& Josh. 1:1–9)	Commissioning successor(s)

16.1—How Matthew Conforms Jesus to Moses the Law-Giver

Mark 14:55f.	Matthew 26:59f. —revising Mark
The chief priests and the whole council sought _____ testimony against Jesus to put him to death; but they found none. For many bore false witness against him, and their witness did not agree.	The chief priests and the whole council sought *false* testimony against Jesus that they might put him to death, but they found none, though many false witnesses came forward.

16.2—How Matthew Makes the Sanhedrin Even More Sinister

Mark 15:15	Matthew 27:24ff.—revising Mark
So Pilate, wishing to satisfy the crowd,	So when Pilate saw that ... a riot was beginning,
	he ... washed his hands before the crowd, saying, *"I am innocent of this man's blood, see to it yourselves."* And all the people answered, *"His blood be on us and on our children!"*
released ... Barabbas; and having scourged Jesus ... delivered him to be crucified.	Then he released ... Barabbas, and having scourged Jesus, delivered him to be crucified.

16.3—Matthew's Insertion of the Blood Curse

16.4—How Matthew Strips Away Camaraderie Reported by Mark

Mark 12:28ff.	Matthew 22:35ff.—revising Mark
One of the scribes ... asked him, "Which commandment is the first of all?"	One of [the Pharisees], a lawyer, asked him a question, ***to test him***. "Teacher, which is the great commandment in the law?"
Jesus answered, "The first is, *'Hear, O Israel: The Lord our God, the Lord is one; and*	And he said to him,_____ _____ _____
you shall love the Lord your God with all your heart, and with all your soul, and with all your mind, and with all your strength.' ..."	You shall love the Lord your God with all your heart, and with all your soul, and with all your mind. This is the great and first commandment....
And the scribe said..., "You are right, Teacher...." Jesus ... said to him, "You are not far from the kingdom of God."	_____ _____ _____ _____

16.5—The Parable of the Marriage Feast (Mt 22:1–14)

First Reading: "The kingdom of heaven may be compared to a king[a] who gave a marriage feast for his son,[b] and sent his servants[c] to call those ... invited[d] ... but they would not come[e].... He sent other servants ... but they made light of it and went ... one to his farm, another to his business,[f] while the rest seized his servants ... and killed them. The king was angry, and he sent his troops[g] and destroyed those murderers and burned their city.[h] Then he said to his servants,[i] 'The wedding is ready, but those invited were not worthy. Go ... to the thoroughfares, and invite ... as many[j] as you find.' And those servants ... gathered all[j] whom they found, both bad and good; so the wedding hall[k] was filled with guests.[l]"

a God	*e Accept that Jesus is*	*j Non-Jews (Gentiles)*
b Celebrating Jesus as	*Messiah*	*— all Jews are already*
Messiah	*f Giving excuses for*	*killed*
c Hebrew prophets	*rejecting Jesus*	*k The Church's ranks*
(later, apostles)	*g Rome's Tenth Legion*	*l Assumed a Gentile-*
d The Jews	*h Jerusalem (in 70)*	*Christian complexion*
	i Apostles (Israel has	
	killed all her prophets)	

Second Reading: "The kingdom of heaven may be compared to God who gave a celebratory feast of recognition that his son, Jesus, is the Messiah, and sent the Hebrew prophets to call the Jews ... but they would not come (i.e., they rejected the proposition that Jesus is the Messiah).... God sent other Hebrew prophets, but some Jews still turned down the request while the rest seized the Hebrew prophets ... and killed them. God was angry, and he sent Rome's Tenth Legion and destroyed the Jews and burned Jerusalem (70 CE). Then God said to the apostles, 'The celebratory feast is ready, but the Jews were not worthy. Go ... to the thoroughfares, and invite ... as many Gentiles as you find.' And the apostles ... gathered all whom they found, both bad and good; this is how the Church's ranks assumed their current Gentile-Christian complexion."

First Reading: "A householder[a] ... planted a vineyard, ... let it out to tenants,[b] and went into another country. When the season of fruit drew near, he sent his servants[c] ... to get his fruit; ... the tenants took his servants ... beat one, killed another, ... stoned another.... He sent other servants ... they did the same to them. Afterward he sent his son[d] ... saying, 'They will respect[e] my son.' But ... the tenants ... said..., 'Let us kill him and have his inheritance' [failing another heir, they assumed the vineyard would be theirs]. And they took him and cast him out of the vineyard, and killed him. When ... the owner ... comes, what will he do to those tenants?" [The Jewish leaders whom Jesus addressed previously] said ... "He will put those wretches to a miserable death,[f] and let out the vineyard[g] to other tenants[h] who will give him ... fruits in their seasons." Jesus said..., "... Therefore ... the kingdom of God [what the "vineyard" means to Matthew] will be taken away from you[b] and given to a nation[h] producing the fruits of it."

a God	d Jesus	g the kingdom of God
b the Jews	e accept him as Messiah	h non-Israel (Gentiles)
c Hebrew prophets	f Rome crushes Jews' revolt (70)	

Second Reading: "God ... planted a vineyard, ... [and] let it out to the Jews.... When the season of fruit drew near, he sent the Hebrew prophets ... to get his fruit; ... the Jews took the Hebrew prophets ... beat one, killed another, ... stoned another.... God sent other Hebrew prophets ... the Jews did the same to them. Afterward God sent his son Jesus ... saying, 'They will accept my son Jesus as Messiah.' But ... the Jews ... said..., 'Let us kill him and have his inheritance.' And the Jews took Jesus and cast him out of the vineyard, and killed him. When ... God ... comes, what will he do to the Jews?" They said ... "God will have Rome crush their revolt (in 70 CE), and let out the kingdom of God to the Gentiles who will give him ... fruits in their seasons." Jesus said..., "... Therefore ... the kingdom of God will be taken away from you Jews and given to Gentiles producing the fruits of it [since what is specified here is another 'nation' i.e., 'non-Israel']."

Mt 10:5–6: "Go nowhere among the ***Gentiles*** [***ethne***], and enter no town of the Samaritans, but go rather to the lost sheep of the house of Israel."	Mt 28:19: "Go and make disciples of all ___?___ [***ethne***]"

16.8—Antioch (Phase I: 30s through 50s)

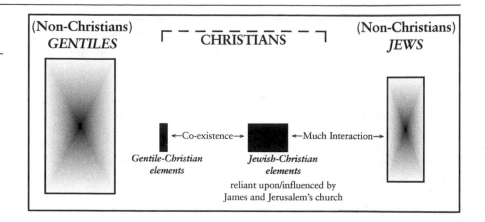

16.9—Antioch (Phase II: from 60 through 70)

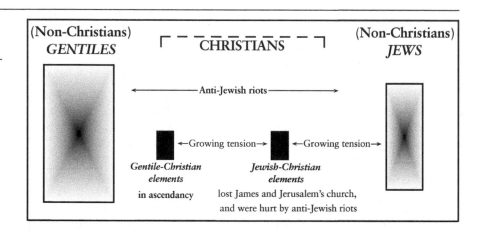

16.10—Antioch (Phase III: the mid-80s)

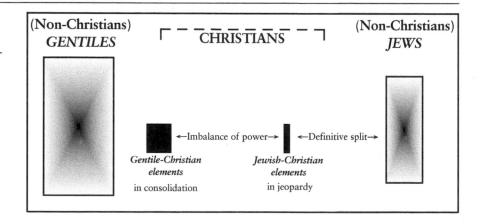

Mark 11:15ff.	Matthew 21:12ff.	Luke 19:45
He entered the temple and began to drive out those who sold and ... bought in the temple, and ...	Jesus entered the temple ... and drove out all who sold and bought in the temple, and ...	He entered the temple and began to drive out those who sold.
overturned the tables of the money-changers and ... seats of those who sold pigeons....	*overturned the tables of the money-changers and ... seats of those who sold pigeons.*	_____ _____ _____ _____

17.1—Luke Dilutes the Temple "Cleansing"

Mark 15:29f.	Matthew 27:40	Luke 23:37
saying, "... *You who would destroy the temple and build it in three days*, save yourself...!"	saying, "*You who would destroy the temple and build it in three days*, save yourself!"	saying, _____ _____ _____ "If you are the King of the Jews, save yourself!"

17.2—Luke Omits Jesus' Temple Threat

18.1—Appearances of the Term "the Jews" (Greek: hoi Ioudaioi) in the Gospels

MARK 6	MATTHEW 5	LUKE 5	JOHN About 70
Independent	*Independent*	*Independent*	*Independent*
7:3	28:15	7:3; 23:50	**At least 39 seemingly hostile:**
			1:19; 2:18,20; 5:10,15,16,18; 6:41,52; 7:1,11,13,15,35; 8:22,48,52,57; 9:12,18,22a, 22b; 10:24,31,33; 11:8,54; 13:33; 18:12,14,31,36,38; 19:7,12,21a,31,38; 20:19
			About 25 other (some possibly hostile):
			2:6,13; 3:1,25; 4:9a,9b,22; 5:1; 6:4; 7:2; 8:31; 10:19; 11:19,31,33,36,45,55; 12:9,11; 18:20,30; 19:14,20,40,42; cf. 18:35
Formulaic "King of the Jews" 15:2,9,12, 18,26	*Formulaic "King of the Jews"* 2:2; 27:11, 29,37	*Formulaic "King of the Jews"* 23:3,37,38	*Formulaic "King of the Jews"* 18:33,39; 19:3,19,21b,21c

18.2—"The Disciples" and "the Jews" as Counterparts in John

JESUS

"THE DISCIPLES"
(Personifying BELIEF)
Sample passages:

"His disciples BELIEVED in him" (2:11).

"His disciples ... BELIEVED ... the word ... Jesus had spoken" (2:22).

"We [the twelve disciples] have BELIEVED, and have come to know, that you are the Holy One of God" (6:68–69).

"[To the disciples Jesus says:] ... BELIEVE in God, BELIEVE also in me.... BELIEVE me that I am in the Father and the Father in me; or else BELIEVE me for the sake of the works themselves.... He who BELIEVES in me will also do the works that I do" (14:1–12).

"His disciples said, '... by this we BELIEVE that you came from God'" (16:29–30).

"THE JEWS"
(Personifying UNBELIEF)
Sample passages:

"How can you [Jews] BELIEVE? ... If you BELIEVED Moses, you would BELIEVE me, for he wrote of me. But if you do not BELIEVE his writing, how will you BELIEVE my words?" (5:44–47).

"I told you [Jews] that you would die in your sins ... unless you BELIEVE that I am he" (8:24).

"Because I tell the truth, you [Jews] do not BELIEVE me.... Why do you not BELIEVE me?" (8:45–46).

"I told you [Jews], and you do not BELIEVE" (10:25–26).

"Though he had done so many signs before [the Jewish crowd] ... they did not BELIEVE in him ... that the word [of] ... Isaiah ... be fulfilled: 'Lord, who has BELIEVED our report ...?' Therefore they could not BELIEVE" (12:37–39).

Figures from Part Six: When Wariness Is Warranted: New Testament Knowledge for Self-Defense

19.1—The Seedliners' "Jewish" Serpent

The *Greek* form (for Nero Caesar)—**Neron Caesar**—in Hebrew transliteration:

Neron | **Caesar** *(Kesar)*

nun (50) + *resh* (200) + *vav* (6) + **nun** (50) + *kuph* (100) + *samekh* (60) + *resh* (200) =   **666**

19.2—Deciphering 666 (and 616) through Gematria

The *Latin* variant (for Nero Caesar)—**Nero_ Caesar**—in Hebrew transliteration:

Nero_ | **Caesar** *(Kesar)*

nun (50) + *resh* (200) + *vav* (6) + _____ + *kuph* (100) + *samekh* (60) + *resh* (200) =   **616**

*Note: The numerical value of Hebrew's "final nun"—present in Nero**n** but not in Nero_—is 50.*

This accounts for the differential between the two variant readings of Revelation's text (666 versus 616).

What Daniel 2 and 7 Mean	How Revelation Misprocesses Daniel
#1 Babylon (6th Century BCE) →	**#1** Babylon (6th Century BCE)
#2 Media (6th Century BCE) →	**#2 Media-Persia (6th Century BCE)**
#3 Persia (6th Century BCE) ↗	**#3** Seleucid Greece (2nd Century BCE) *Reign of Antiochus IV*
#4 Seleucid Greece (2nd Century BCE) *Reign of Antiochus IV* ↗	**#4** [room now for] **Rome!** (1st Century CE) *Reign of Domitian (81–96 CE)*

19.3—How Daniel's Four Empires Were Misprocessed by Revelation

Figures from Part Seven: Integrating Matters

21.1—Marcan Insertions That Impacted Jewish History

What Mark Does →	Why Mark Does It →	What Results →	*Reversing* the Process
Mark inserts a **"blasphemy"** unit (2:5b–10) into the healing of the paralytic	to prepare readers for "blasphemy" as Jesus' Sanhedrin verdict (Fig. 12.9).	His insertion destroys the logic of the paralytic story (Fig. 12.10).	No sooner do we subtract this unit than a cohesive story resurfaces (see Chap. 12).
Mark inserts a **"Passover"** unit (14:12–16) before the Last Supper	to alter an ordinary meal into a Passover observance.	His insertion (Fig. 10.2) creates up to five glaring incongruities.	No sooner do we subtract this unit than the incongruities vanish and a consistent storyline reappears (Chap. 10).
Mark inserts a **"Sanhedrin"** unit (that developed in layers) between 14:53 and 15:1 (Fig. 12.3) so	a "consultation" (15:1) becomes a trial, *Jewish* (not Roman) officials are blamed for Jesus' conviction, and "blasphemy" displaces sedition as the charge against him.	The layered elements are artificial and not cohesive (Fig. 12.2), and Mark's editing creates a factual error (in 15:1).	No sooner do we subtract this unit than the error vanishes and a cohesive storyline reappears (Chap. 12).
Mark inserts a **"Barabbas"** unit—with its prisoner release—between 15:5 and 15:15b	(among other reasons) to defuse the charge that Jesus was a seditionist ("The King of the Jews").	His insertion makes arresting the popular Jesus seem illogical (cf. Jesus' greeting on Palm Sunday).	No sooner do we subtract this unit than the illogic vanishes and a consistent storyline resumes (Chap. 12)

22.1—Anti-Judaism in the New Testament Is Denied

I Defensive Arguments by Some Christians	II My Reactions
I a) Inspired by God and reflecting divine love, the New Testament could not have been intended to encourage contempt of any people. Since Jesus spoke this language of love, preaching the turning of the other cheek, even loving one's enemies, those recording his teachings, and deeply committed to him themselves, could hardly have written works that are anti-Jewish.	**II a)** Since Jews do not include the New Testament among their sacred texts, any argument proceeding, as if self-evidently, from the New Testament's divine inspiration will not be persuasive. Moreover, that Jesus himself spoke the language of love hardly guarantees that those committed to him (including the Gospels' editors themselves) did so as well.
I b) The New Testament's apparently harsh language against Jews is simply prophetic rebuke out of love. Just as the Hebrew prophets, reprimanding Israelites of their day, are not to be judged anti-Jewish, neither should Jesus' criticisms of Jews be so construed. These were a kind of oratorical style or literary device not intended as final but merely to shock people into repentance before it was too late.	**II b)** Gospel condemnations of Jews exceed reprimands by the Hebrew prophets. The latter intended to solidify covenantal bonds between God and the Jews whereas New Testament censure of Jews warns of God's replacing them with *others*! Jesus may have scolded fellow Jews out of love, but the ferocity *ascribed* to him reflects sentiments of later Gospel editors, and is so prominently displayed that it must be judged anti-Jewish.
I c) The Gospels and book of Acts show us, approvingly, thousands of Jews accepting Jesus' message, or at least eager to hear what he had said. How, then, when the New Testament presents, with acclaim, so many Jews so positively disposed toward Jesus' message and Jesus' following, can modern Jews deem the New Testament anti-Jewish?	**II c)** The Gospels and Acts, while not biased against all Jews, are biased against *Jews rejecting Jesus*, not opposed to Jews accepting Jesus but condemnatory of those who do not—and it is the latter with whom modern Jews identify.
I d) The church fathers' denunciations of Jews date from later times when the Church began forging weapons for its conflict with Judaism. Only *then* did interpreters of the sacred gospel apply their own personal biases against Jews to the non-prejudicial truths of the New Testament itself.	**II d)** Just as the church fathers superimposed their own later attitudes onto earlier views of the New Testament itself, so also did the four Evangelists themselves—in producing and editing these Gospels—convey and superimpose their own anti-Jewish sentiments in the very process of depicting both Jesus and his ministry.

22.2—Anti-Judaism in the New Testament Is Minimized

III Defensive Arguments by Some Christians	IV My Reactions
III a) Other ancient literatures attacked opponents. Certain New Testament polemics are even comparatively mild! That these diatribes were conventions of a bygone era frees us to dismiss them as irrelevant for modern times.	**IV a)** Christians today are not sufficiently conversant with conventions of ancient polemic to bring them to bear in evaluating the New Testament, which, moreover, they distinguish from most other ancient writings as the *inspired word of God*, an authority that offsets any putative mildness.
III b) Authors of New Testament writings were not conscious of contributing to a new biblical corpus. Jewish scripture was the only Bible they envisioned. Had they known the importance their writings would assume, and the possible detrimental effect their words might have on the Jews, such authors would have tempered their presentation of the Jewish people.	**IV b)** To suggest that such awareness would have induced them to abstain from using abusive language, or at least to tone it down, is conjectural and does not address *realities* at hand. When later Christian authorities did realize the negativity toward Jews in, e.g., the Gospels, some intensified it in their own writings!
III c) The New Testament's apparent anti-Jewish polemic was actually only "in-house" squabbling between Jews who accepted Jesus over against others who had not. Thus, even post-70, when Gospels were being composed, anti-Jewish polemics turn out only to be by *Christian* Jews against *fellow* Jews, not polemics by non-Jews against Jews.	**IV c)** Increasingly, after 70, churches were becoming severed from the "Synagogue," with most Christians not "in" the Jewish house at all (Chaps. 16 and 21). The "in-house squabbling" argument, while popular, convenient, and comforting, is not always soundly based and results in some unnatural readings of Gospel texts.
III d) Since Jews "gave" Christians Jesus and Paul, the twelve apostles*, and Jewish scripture, Christian expressions of negativity cannot extend deeply lest Christians cut into their own foundation in Judaism. Seemingly harsh rebuke of Jews could better be construed as exasperation *on behalf of* Jews who have not recognized the fulfillment of their own heritage. This is hardly bias!	**IV d)** The core issue operative here is that, since the Jews gave the world the concept of the Messiah, the Jews should also be best qualified to identify that Messiah. In failing to accept Jesus, Jews denied the core of Christian theology. Far more than mere exasperation is involved here.

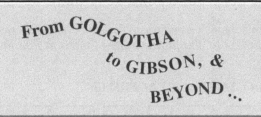

Figure 23.1

TRUTH IN PASSION PRODUCTIONS?
"What is truth?"—Pilate (Jn 18:38)

Suitability Index for Using This Multipurpose Book: Matching Contents to Occasion

Note: *Shaded* indicates appropriate for that audience. *Not shaded* means less appropriate.
Key: B—"Before We Proceed"; I—"Introduction"; N—"Notes on Terminology"

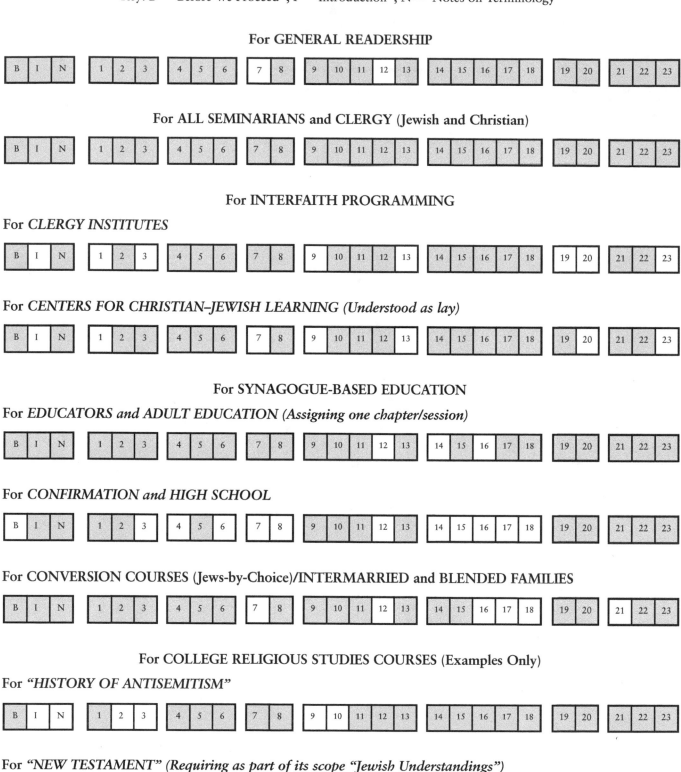

About *Modern Jews Engage the New Testament: Enhancing Jewish Well-Being in a Christian Environment*

An honest, probing look at the dynamics of the New Testament—in relation to problems that disconcert Jews and Christians today.

Despite the New Testament's impact on Jewish history, virtually all Jews avoid knowledge of its underlying dynamics. Jewish families and communities thus remain needlessly stymied when responding to a deeply Christian culture. Their Christian friends, meanwhile, are left perplexed as to why Jews are wary of the Gospel's "good news."

This long-awaited volume offers an unprecedented solution-oriented introduction to Jesus and Paul, the Gospels and Revelation, leading Jews out of anxieties that plague them, and clarifying for Christians why Jews draw back from Christians' sacred writings.

Accessible to lay people, scholars and clergy of all faiths, innovative teaching aids make this valuable resource ideal for rabbis, ministers and other educators. Topics include:

- The Gospels, Romans and Revelation— the Key Concerns for Jews
- Misusing the Talmud in Gospel Study
- Jesus' Trial, the "Virgin Birth" and Empty Tomb Enigmas
- Millennialist Scenarios and Missionary Encroachment
- The Last Supper and Church Seders
- Is the New Testament Antisemitic?

While written primarily with Jews in mind, this groundbreaking volume will also help Christians understand issues involved in the origin of the New Testament, the portrayal of Judaism in it, and why for centuries their "good news" has been a source of fear and mistrust among Jews.

For People of All Faiths, All Backgrounds

JEWISH LIGHTS Publishing
www.jewishlights.com

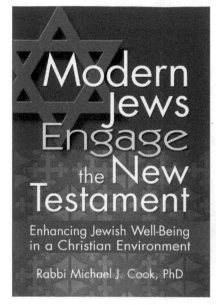

6 x 9, 416 pp, Hardcover
ISBN-13: 978-1-58023-313-2
ISBN-10: 1-58023-313-9

"A wonderful resource for Jews who seek to take on the challenges posed by the New Testament and for Christians who wish to understand Jews' relationship to Christian theology. Whether for individual or group study, [its] educational value is without measure."
—**Rabbi Eric H. Yoffie**, president, Union for Reform Judaism

"Superb. Builds on Cook's mastery of sound New Testament scholarship with innovative interpretations and lucid [expression].... Useful for laity, clergy and scholars, [and] essential for [those] dedicated to Christian-Jewish dialogue."
—**Joseph B. Tyson**, professor emeritus of religious studies, Southern Methodist University; author, *Marcion and Luke-Acts: A Defining Struggle*

"Covers the highlights of the Gospels and New Testament Christianity and makes [readers new to the topic] feel more at home. Useful for all engaged in Jewish and Christian dialogue."
—**Rabbi Burton L. Visotzky**, Appleman Professor of Midrash and Interreligious Studies, The Jewish Theological Seminary; author, *A Delightful Compendium of Consolation*

"Practical, pointed and provocative.... Points out how and why Jews need to understand this material. A welcome addition to both New Testament scholarship and Jewish-Christian relations."
—**Amy-Jill Levine**, E. Rhodes and Leona B. Carpenter Professor of New Testament Studies, Vanderbilt University Divinity School

Printed in the USA
CPSIA information can be obtained
at www.ICGtesting.com
JSHW060049150824
68134JS00031B/2684